First World War
and Army of Occupation
War Diary
France, Belgium and Germany

58 DIVISION
174 Infantry Brigade
London Regiment
7th (City of London) Battalion
1 February 1918 - 30 November 1918

WO95/3005/6

The Naval & Military Press Ltd
www.nmarchive.com
Published in association with The National Archives

Published by

The Naval & Military Press Ltd

Unit 10 Ridgewood Industrial Park,

Uckfield, East Sussex,

TN22 5QE England

Tel: +44 (0) 1825 749494

www.naval-military-press.com

www.nmarchive.com

This diary has been reprinted in facsimile from the original. Any imperfections are inevitably reproduced and the quality may fall short of modern type and cartographic standards.

© Crown Copyright
Images reproduced by permission of The National Archives, London, England, 2015.

Contents

Document type	Place/Title	Date From	Date To
Heading	WO95/3005/6		
Heading	58 Division 174 Bde 1/7 London Regt 1918 Feb-1918 Nov From 47 Div 140 Bde Absorbed 2/7 Bn 1918 Feb		
War Diary	Domart	01/02/1918	08/02/1918
War Diary	Buttes De Rouy	09/02/1918	09/02/1918
War Diary	Anigmy-Rouy	10/02/1918	26/02/1918
War Diary	Buttes De Rouy	27/02/1918	27/02/1918
War Diary	Pierremande	28/02/1918	31/03/1918
Heading	174th Inf. Bde. 58th Div War Diary 7th Battn. The London Regiment April 1918		
War Diary		01/04/1918	31/05/1918
Operation(al) Order(s)	7th Battn. London Regt. Order No. 2	09/05/1918	09/05/1918
Operation(al) Order(s)	7 Battalion Order No. 3		
Operation(al) Order(s)	7 Battn Order No. 4	22/05/1918	22/05/1918
Operation(al) Order(s)	7 Battalion Order No. 5		
Operation(al) Order(s)	Battalion Order No. 6	31/05/1918	31/05/1918
War Diary	Baizieux	01/06/1918	04/06/1918
War Diary	Daily Mail Woods	05/06/1918	09/06/1918
War Diary	Picquigny	10/06/1918	15/06/1918
War Diary	Baizieux	16/06/1918	19/06/1918
War Diary	In Line	20/06/1918	30/06/1918
War Diary	Baizieux	01/07/1918	01/07/1918
War Diary	Albert	01/07/1918	13/07/1918
War Diary	Baizieux	13/07/1918	18/07/1918
War Diary	Albert	18/07/1918	30/07/1918
War Diary	Round Camp Wood	30/07/1918	02/08/1918
War Diary	Halloy	03/08/1918	04/08/1918
War Diary	Bonnay	05/08/1918	05/08/1918
War Diary	In Line	06/08/1918	10/08/1918
War Diary	Bray-Corbie Road	11/08/1918	12/08/1918
War Diary	Round Wood	13/08/1918	31/08/1918
Heading	174th Bde 58th Div 7th Battalion London Regiment August 1918		
Miscellaneous	7th Battn. The London Regiment Narrative of Operations 8th. 9th. and 10th August 1918	10/08/1918	10/08/1918
Miscellaneous	7th Battalion The London Regiment Narrative Of Operations August 25th To September 1st 1918	01/09/1918	01/09/1918
War Diary	Hem Wood	01/09/1918	11/09/1918
War Diary	Lieramont	12/09/1918	21/09/1918
War Diary	Ronsoy	22/09/1918	30/09/1918
Miscellaneous	7th Battalion The London Regiment Narrative Of Operations 6th To 11th September 1918	11/09/1918	11/09/1918
War Diary	M 6 a 8.4	01/10/1918	02/10/1918
War Diary	Hythe Tunnel	02/10/1918	03/10/1918
War Diary	Halibut Trench H34 a4.6	03/10/1918	11/10/1918
War Diary	Lievin	12/10/1918	12/10/1918
War Diary	O15d.8.9	12/10/1918	15/10/1918
War Diary	Courrieres	15/10/1918	16/10/1918
War Diary	J 25d.7.4	16/10/1918	17/10/1918
War Diary	J28 Central	17/10/1918	17/10/1918

War Diary	K 27a.6.4	17/10/1918	18/10/1918
War Diary	L13d4.2	19/10/1918	19/10/1918
War Diary	Vert Bois	19/10/1918	19/10/1918
War Diary	Nomain	20/10/1918	27/10/1918
War Diary	Cense De Choques	28/10/1918	28/10/1918
War Diary	J9d1.5	29/10/1918	07/11/1918
War Diary	Maulde Mortagne	08/11/1918	08/11/1918
War Diary	Brasmenil	09/11/1918	09/11/1918
War Diary	Beloeil	10/11/1918	10/11/1918
War Diary	Grosage	11/11/1918	12/11/1918
War Diary	Beloeil	13/11/1918	30/11/1918
Map	Map 'A'		

WO 95/3005/6

58 Division

174 BDE

1/7 London Regt

1918 FEB - 1918 NOV

FROM 47 DIV 140 BDE

ABSORBED 2/7 BN 1918 FEB

WAR DIARY
or
INTELLIGENCE SUMMARY.

(Erase heading not required.)

Army Form C. 2118.

Instructions regarding War Diaries and Intelligence Summaries are contained in F. S. Regs., Part II. and the Staff Manual respectively. Title pages will be prepared in manuscript.

7 London Regt

Place	Date	Hour	Summary of Events and Information	Remarks and references to Appendices
DOMART	1.2.18		Company Training.	
	2.2.18		Following officers, v 165 O.R., joined from 17th Battalion The London Regt. for amalgamation.	
			CAPT. J.G.H. BUDD.	
			A/CAPT. L.E. BISHOP M.C.	
			A/CAPT. C.J. METCALF	
			A/CAPT. V.H. RABY.	
			LT. R.G. MILLER	
			2/LT. J.F. PRESTON M.C.	
			2/LT. C. FEATHERSTONE	
			2/LT. H.H. HARTNAM	
			Amalgamated Battalion henceforth known as 7th Batt. The LONDON Regt.	
	3.2.18		Reorganisation. Church Parade. MAJOR W. HUNT and 1 officer per Coy proceeded to reconnoitre line to be taken over.	
			LT. COL. S.L. HOSKING rejoined from leave.	
	4.2.18		Company Training. Reorganisation.	
	5.2.18		Company Training.	
	6.2.18		Company Training. MAJOR WHITEHEAD D.S.O. rejoined for duty as Second-in-Command.	
	7.2.18		Company Training. Part of Transport started for new area & moved route.	
	8.2.18		Battalion marched from DOMART to VILLERS BRETONNEUX & entrained. Detrained at APPILLY; moved by route to SINCENY; thence by march route to BOITE DE ROUY, relieving 18th MANCHESTERS as D Battalion of 90 Brigade. Two Coys & Transport billeted in SINCENY.	Sheet ST. QUENTIN 1/100,000
BOITES DE ROUY	9.2.18		Battalion relieved 17th MANCHESTERS in left sub-sector of Brigade front; relief complete 11-59 p.m.	O.O. 4
			Dispositions as follows:- Batt. H.Q. in ANIGNY ROUY (B24 d74)	O.O. 5
			D Coy Left front.	Sheet 70 D.N.W. 1/20,000
			B " Right "	
			A " Left Support (Counter attack Coy)	
			C " Right Support (Counter defence Coy)	

1577 Wt.W10791/1773 500,000 1/15 D. D. & L. A.D.S.S./Forms/C. 2118.

WAR DIARY or INTELLIGENCE SUMMARY

Army Form C. 2118.

(Erase heading not required.)

Instructions regarding War Diaries and Intelligence Summaries are contained in F. S. Regs., Part II. and the Staff Manual respectively. Title pages will be prepared in manuscript.

Place	Date	Hour	Summary of Events and Information	Remarks and references to Appendices
ANIGNY-ROUY	10.2.18		In line. App.	
	12.2.18		In line. App.	
	13.2.18		Inter-Company relief. A Coy. relieved D; C Coy relieved B; D & B Coys. took up positions previously occupied by A & C respectively. Relief complete 9-30 p.m. App.	O.O.6.
	14.2.18		In line. App.	
	16.2.18			
	17.2.18		Inter-company relief. D Coy relieved A, B relieved C; A & C Coys took previous positions of D & B respectively. App.	O.O.7.
	18.2.18		In line. App.	
	20.2.18			
	21.2.18		Inter-company relief. App.	
	22.2.18		In line. App.	
	24.2.18		Lt.Col. HOSKING to 7th Army C.O.; Comm. Major HUNT M.C. in command. 6 officers joined Battn. from Reinforcement Camp.	
	25.2.18		Battalion relieved in line by 9th LONDONS. Relief complete 9-30 p.m. App.	
	26.2.18		Battalion moved to BUTTES DE ROUY (HQ A & C Coys) and SINCENY (B & D Coys), taking over from 9th LONDONS and becoming Reserve left Batte Zone Battalion of sector. App.	O.O.8.
BUTTES DE ROUY	27.2.18		Battalion relieved in SINCENY and BUTTES DE ROUY by 10th LONDONS. Relief complete 11-50 a.m. Battalion relieved 4th LONDONS in Right Batte zone position. Relief complete 3 p.m. Disposition as follows:— A.Q., C Coy., A Coy (less 1 Platoon) PIERREMANDE. B (less 1 Platoon) UZOF. D Coy BERNAGOUSSE QUARRY.	O.O.9.
PIERREMANDE	28.2.18		C Coy. moved from PIERREMANDE to relieve 2 companies 8th LONDONS in BERNAGOUSSE QUARRIES. D Coy. & 1 Platoon B Coy. relieved front line.	

Army Form C. 2118.

WAR DIARY
or
INTELLIGENCE SUMMARY.
(Erase heading not required.)

Instructions regarding War Diaries and Intelligence Summaries are contained in F. S. Regs., Part II. and the Staff Manual respectively. Title pages will be prepared in manuscript.

Place	Date	Hour	Summary of Events and Information	Remarks and references to Appendices
PIERREMANDE	28.2.18	2.10pm	Message received from 174th Brigade: TAKE PRECAUTIONARY ACTION	
		4.30pm	Reported to 174 Bde that Precautionary Action had been taken.	

Army Form C. 2118.

WAR DIARY
or
INTELLIGENCE SUMMARY.

1/4 London Regt

(Erase heading not required.)

Place	Date	Hour	Summary of Events and Information	Remarks and references to Appendices
	1.3.16		Battalion Relieved in Right Battle Zone by 6th London Relief complete by 6 p.m. 1931	O.O. 10.
	2.3.16		Battalion Relieved B. Coy Section in Line. Relief complete midnight. 1931	
	3.3.16			
	4.3.16		In Line. 1931	
	5.3.16			
	6.3.16		Major S.L. looking returned from 5th Army School	
	7.3.16		Relieved in Line by 5th London. proceeded to billets in PERRENANDE	O.O.11.
	8.3.16		Bn in Divisional Reserve 1931	
	9.3.16			
	10.3.16			
	11.3.16		Working Parties + Rifleting. 1931	
	12.3.16			
	13.3.16			
	14.3.16			
	15.3.16			
	16.3.16		Relieve 6th London in Line Relief complete midnight. 1934	
	17.3.16		In line 1931 on account of pending trench attack. 1931	
	18.3.16		In line. Enemy attacked one of our posts nearly 2 of our own memory hits	
	19.3.16		In line. 1931	
	20.3.16		In line. 1931	
	21.3.16		In line 1931	
	22.3.16		In line. Enemy attempted to raid one of our posts, parole own recapture the Officer leader 1931	
	23.3.16		In line. " " " " " Enemy left barn. 1931	
	24.3.16		In line 1931	
	25.3.16		In line 1931	
	26.3.16		In line 1931	
	27.3.16		were encouraged. the Bn taking over the Battle zone from 6th London relieved C + D Coys 1931	
	28.3.16		A + B Coys + Second by B.V.C. A + B Coys move to ST. PAUL	
	29.3.16		A + B Coys relieved by B.V.C. & also C + D move to ST. PAUL relieved in billets by 6.30 a.m. 31.3.16	O.O. 13
	30.3.16			
	31.3.16			

364

174th Inf.Bde.
58th Div.

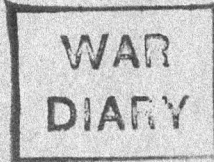

7th BATTN. THE LONDON REGIMENT.

A P R I L

1 9 1 8

WAR DIARY or INTELLIGENCE SUMMARY

Army Form C. 2118.

Place: 7th London Rgt.

Date 1918	Hour	Summary of Events and Information	Remarks and references to Appendices
April 1		Grand Hôtel Doctor.	
" 2		Returned hp 38. Highland Inf Bgd. then proceeded by March route to VIC SUR AISNE entrained at 6 pm for LONGEAU	
" 3		Detrained at LONGEAU, time 12.30 pm. Reported to 16th Division (endeavouring to get linked with 58th Division) proceeded by March route to BOVES. Billeted for night, received orders from 16th Division to meet B.G.C. 9th Queen's Bde next day ½ at GENTELLES to arrange relief of that Bde on the night 4/5th	
" 4		Received orders timed 10.40 am for Bn to move at once, to GENTELLES WOOD, as divisional reserve, first platoon moved off 11.40 am. Battalion in position 1 pm. During afternoon received orders to take up position astride LONGEAU VILLERS BRETONNEUX Road. & came under orders of 42nd Bde 24th Division.	
" 5		In position astride of reserve astride LONGEAU VILLERS BRETONNEUX Road. during late afternoon came under orders of 18 Division, ordered to extend line to the south to a point where the great line separated the O squares from the U squares	
" 6		In position as for night of 5 met came under orders of 58th Division	
" 7		"	
" 8		"	
" 9		Ammn was supplied Battalion within Boundary	
" 10			
" 11		Ammn was supplied during Battalion within Boundary	
" 12		Runners of B B " A " " C " B " & Coys. with HQrs to BLANGY-WOOD then on relief by 59th Bn A.I.F - H? Coy Rest Bn further went Loy.	

WAR DIARY
or
INTELLIGENCE SUMMARY.
(Erase heading not required.)

Instructions regarding War Diaries and Intelligence Summaries are contained in F. S. Regs., Part II. and the Staff Manual respectively. Title pages will be prepared in manuscript.

Place	Date	Hour	Summary of Events and Information	Remarks and references to Appendices
	13th		The Battn. moved forward from 6th LONDON REGT. and were in Bde. reserve.	Ref. map Sheet 62d.
	14th/15th		In reserve at 0340.	
	16th		The Battn. relieved 6th LONDON REGT in the line in front of VILLERS-BRETONNEUX inclusive V16 87 to VILLERS-BRETONNEUX — WARFUSEE road exclusive P25d 22. holding from railway. Relief complete 10.45pm. Dispositions as follows:— D Coy right front Coy C " centre " " B " left " " A " Support & Counter attack Coy. Bn. HQ. in VILLERS-BRETONNEUX 035 631	
	17th		on fire	
	18th		" "	
	19th		night 19.20th relieved by 8th Northants Withdrew to ~~Brewery~~ BOUTILLERIE	
	20th		as above	
	21st		Reorganisation & refitting	
	22nd		— ditto —	
	23rd		— ditto —	
	24th		Standing by to "Prepare for attack". Orders received to "however" Battalion moved to however position awaiting orders. D.O.M.G. joined for duty and took over command of B Coy	

INTELLIGENCE SUMMARY

Instructions regarding War Diaries and Intelligence Summaries are contained in F. S. Regs., Part II. and the Staff Manual respectively. Title pages will be prepared in manuscript.

(Erase heading not required.)

Place	Date	Hour	Summary of Events and Information	Remarks and references to Appendices
	25th	11.30 A	{15th Infantry Bde.} Relieved by the French, 7 Battalion withdrew to reserve position, proceeded to relieve the 3rd Batth. London Regt (relief complete 19, midnight-) in CACHY SECTOR	
	26th		" "	
	27th		" " Relieved by the French night " " 28th. 0 Battalion withdrew to N 32 C Sheet 62 D SW.	
	28th		Proceeded by bus to CAOURS arrived in billets 7-30 pm	
	29th		Reorganisation - refitting. Capt: o : O filled vac. Comdg H.Q.L Jackson Lieut (to A Payments) joined for duty.	
	30th		Training and Inspections	

W. Mitchell
Captain
Commanding

WAR DIARY
or
~~INTELLIGENCE SUMMARY~~

(Erase heading not required.)

Army Form C. 2118.

17/5/8 7 Fusiliers 17

Place	Date	Hour	Summary of Events and Information	Remarks and references to Appendices
La Vallée	1-5-18		CAOURS. Training - Close Order drill, Lewis Gun, Stretcher bearers classes.	
	2-5-18		– ditto –	
	3-5-18		– ditto –	
	4-5-18		– ditto –	
	5-5-18		– ditto –	
	6-5-18		Battalion billeted at junction of roads leading to NEUF MOULIN and ABBEVILLE - ST RIQUIER.	
	7-5-18		Road for MOUFLIERS AU BOIS. Arrived in Billets 6-30 pm.	
	8.P.M.		On 10 PM at MOUFLIERS AU BOIS. Battalion standing by ready to move at 1 hour notice	
	8-5-18		Moved by March route to MIRVAUX - Arrived in Billets at Mirvaux 7-30 pm	
	9-5-18		Company and Platoon training - Battalion in the Counter attack	Bn Order No 2.
	10-5-18		" "	
	11-5-18		Proceeded by March route to V.28.d. Sheet 57.D NW. Arrived at 9-30 pm. New Battle Camp	Bn Order No 2.
	12-5-18		Battalion on Working parties	
	13-5-18		" "	
	14-5-18		" "	
	15-5-18		Proceeded to firing line relieved 21st Indon Regt. C & D Coys front line A & B support to 8 Millencourt	Bn Orders No 3
	16-5-18		Battalion in line. Headquarters moved to V.30.b. H.9. Sheet 62.D.	
	17-5-18		" "	
	18-5-18		" " Patrols to Quarry. -	
	19-5-18		" " Working and Carrying parties	
	20-5-18		Night of 19/20 relieved by 8th battalion The Gordon Regt. A & B Companies withdraw to MELBOURNE trench C, D and H.Q. to HENNECOURT.	
	21-5-18		1AM C. D. + H.Q. moved from HENNECOURT to battle positions, withdrew at 4 AM	
	22-5-18		Inter Company reliefs. C & D relieved A & B Companies	

38 / sheets

Army Form C. 2118.

WAR DIARY
or
INTELLIGENCE SUMMARY.
(Erase heading not required.)

Instructions regarding War Diaries and Intelligence Summaries are contained in F. S. Regs., Part II. and the Staff Manual respectively. Title pages will be prepared in manuscript.

Place	Date	Hour	Summary of Events and Information	Remarks and references to Appendices
	22.5.18		Battalion in Brigade Support - Working and Carrying Parties	
	23.5.18		Battalion moved into line from HENNECOURT and MELBOURNE trench relieving 6th London Regiment on the RIGHT SECTOR of the MILLENCOURT SECTOR. A and B front Companies C support D reserve Companies	7 Bn Order No H.
	24.5.18		On the line - Working parties and Patrols.	
	25.5.18		" "	
	26.6.18		" "	
	27.5.18		" "	
	27.5.18		Night 27/28 relieved by 9th London Regiment. Battalion to HENNECOURT WOOD. 26.9 to V26.a.9 Sheet 57.D	7 Bn Order No 5.
	28.5.18		as Battalion in Divisional Reserve.	
	29.5.18		Standing by. Battalion ready to move at 1 hours notice Inspection of Lewis Guns and rifles by Commander Sergeant. Working parties in SYDNEY TRENCH	
	30.5.18		Morning - Enemy commenced shelling at 2.7AM to 3.15AM. Battalion withdrew to Alternative Position - Casualties Officers - 2/Lt J. Vaughan Russell Wounded. O Ranks 4 Killed 21 Wounded. 4.30 pm Battalion proceeded to BAIZIEUX SYSTEM taking over from 7th Buffs.	7 Bn Order to 6

K W Mumman
Lieut Colonel Manchester

7th Battn. London Regt Orders No 2.

9-5-18   Ref Sheet No 57D - 62D 1/40,000

I Move. (a) The Battalion will move today to U 28 d. by route
B 2 b and d — BEAUCOURT — CONTAY ROAD.
(b) Headquarters and Companies will pass the starting point
road junction immediately South of the M in MIRVAUX
as follows :— "C" Company 10-35 AM. "D" Company 10-40 AM
H Q 10-45 AM "B" Company 10-50 AM Transport 11 AM
(c) 50 yards interval will be maintained between platoons
halts will be taken from Head of Column.

II 2/Lieut H L Woolner will report at Battalion Orderly Room at
9 AM and will proceed on horseback to CONTAY where
he will report to the Staff Captain at CONTAY church
U 27 a 3.5 at 10-30 AM. Transport Officer will arrange
necessary chargers.

III Tents The 7 tents in possession will be struck by the Stepping
platoon and returned by Quartermaster to Brigade
Quartermasters Stores by 10-30 AM

IV Lewis Guns Etc (a) Lewis Guns SAA (sufficient to supply each man with
the 50 extra rounds) Signal Equipment, Tools, Cookers
and Water Carts will accompany Battalion.
(b) Tools will be dumped in new area and animals
and limbers returned to MIRVAUX

V Valises Etc (a) Officers valises and mess boxes will be dumped
at QM Stores by 9 AM
(b) Companies will return the extra 50 rounds per man
to QM Stores by 8-30 AM
(c) Medical stores will be packed on Maltese Cart
and ready to move with remainder of transport

VI QM Stores Etc — Quartermasters Stores and Transport lines
will remain in present position

VII Billets Quartermaster will hand over accommodation and
Billets to a Battalion of the 173rd Brigade

Sgd S O Peppiatt Capt & Adjt

7 Battalion Order No 2.   Copy No

SECRET

Ref 57D 62D 1/40,000

1. 7th Battalion will relieve the 21st Battalion in the left sub sector of the right (MILLENCOURT) sector on night of 15th/16th inst. in accordance with attached schedule.

2. Companies will move off as follows:- Transport 4-20 PM C Company 4-30 PM D Company 4-35 PM "B" Company 4-40 PM "A" Company 4-45 PM Sapping Platoon and Aid Post 4-50 PM Remainder of Headquarters 4-55 PM Platoons will move at 50 yards distance. Route Road Bend V.26.a.9.6.

3. One Officer 2 N.C.O's per Company R.S.M, Signalling Sergt 2 Signallers & Runners & Snipers will report to the Intelligence Officer at Guard Room at 1 PM and will proceed to Forward Area to take over stores and accommodation. Receipts for Trench Stores taken over will be forwarded to B.O.R. by 12 noon 16th inst.

4. No cooking will be done in the lines except by means of Tommy's Cookers. Rations for Companies will be sent up each night to W.25.c.1.4 Necessary carrying parties being provided by the Reserve Company. Rations for HQ will be dumped at Battalion Headquarters.

5. Officers valises, Mess Boxes etc will be dumped outside Guard Room by 5-30 PM for conveyance to Q. M. Stores

6. Code Word for relief complete "LONDON"

7. Lewis Guns and Mess Sandbags of the Companies will be dumped at HENNECOURT CHATEAU. Headquarters Lewis Guns and Mess Sand Bags will be dumped at BHQ

SCHEDULE

7th Bn	21st London	Guides	Time	Place	Remarks
"C" Coy relieves	"A"	1 Per Platoon 1 C.H. Qtrs	9-0 PM	HENNECOURT CHATEAU	Left Front Coy
"D" relieve	"D"	ditto	ditto		Right " "
"B" "	"C"	ditto	ditto		Support "
"A" "	"B"	ditto	ditto		Reserve "
Sapping platoon & Aid Post		1	ditto		V 30 d
Remainder of HQ		1	ditto		MILLENCOURT V 29 d.1.4

DISTRIBUTION NORMAL

W.O. Peppiatt
Capt & Adjt

<u>Secret</u>　　　7th. Battn. Order No. 4.　　　d/22-5-18.
Ref. Sheets 57D 62D 1/20000　　　　　　Copy No. 12

1. 7th. Battn. will relieve 6th. Battn. in right sub-section of Brigade Front tomorrow night May 23/24 in accordance with attached schedule. 'A' Coy. will leave HENENCOURT 9.15 pm 'B' Coy. 9.20 pm.

2. Work under R.E's. will be carried out by whole Battn. (less covering parties, patrol and carrying parties) immediately on completion of relief. Details regarding rendezvous etc. will be issued later. Capt. Symonds will be responsible that adequate covering parties are provided.

3. (a) Company Commanders & C.S.M's of 'A' and 'B' Coys. will report to 6th. Bn. H.Q. MILLENCOURT at 4.30 p.m where they will be provided with guides and will proceed to reconnoitre their new front, arrange accommodation and take over stores

(b) Company Commanders & C.S.M's of 'C' and 'D' Coys. will report at their new Coy. H.Q.'s at dusk for reconnaissance as their line cannot be reconnoitred during the hours of daylight.

4. Rations and water for the Bn. will be sent up as follows:-
    H.Q. to Battn H.Q. V30 b 4.5
A and B Coys to front line by pack ponies via MILLENCOURT-ALBERT road. 'C' Coy limbers to KING ST via MILLENC'T-ALBERT road. 'D' Coy limbers to QUEEN ST. via MILLENC'T-ALBERT road. Rations should reach their dumps at 1 a.m. Coys. will arrange necessary carrying parties.

5. Lewis Guns and mess sand-bags of HQ, 'A' and 'B' Coys will be dumped outside their respective HQ by 8.20 p.m. and will all be taken up to dump V30 b 3.5 near Bn HQ where they will be picked up by H.Q. & Coys on their way in.

6. (a) No petrol cans will be handed over on relief with the exception of Bde. Reserve. HQ, 'A'&'B' Coys will dump petrol cans at Bn. H.Q by 6 pm. 'C'&'D' Coys. will move their cans to the new area. If this is not strictly

2/

carried out arrangements for an adequate supply of water to Coys. becomes impossible.

(b) Receipts for trench stores handed over and taken over (including tools) will be sent to HQ by 12 noon 24th. inst.

7. 6th. Battn. will take over present positions of 7th. Bn. Guide from A & B Coys will meet advanced party of 6th. Bn. at HENENCOURT CHATEAU gates at 6 p.m.

2 Guides each from C & D Coys. will report to A & B Coy HQ of 6th. Bn. at 9.30 p.m. to guide the Coys of the 6th. Bn to their new positions.

8. Relief complete will be notified by name of Coy. Cmdr. concerned, being wired to Battalion H.Q.

Signed. H. O. Peppiatte.
Capt. & / Adjt.

SCHEDULE

7th. Bn.	Relieved by 8th. Bn.	Guides.	Time.	Place	Remarks
H.Q	H.Q.	—	—	—	C/i 8th. Bn HQ MURRAY TRENCH (V30 a 4.5)
A. Coy.	C. Coy	1 per platoon	10 pm.	Junction of AUSTRALIA & MURRAY TR. V30 a 4.4	Right Front Company
B. Coy	D. Coy	ditto	ditto.		Left Front Coy.
C. Coy	A. Coy	2 guides	9.30 pm C Coy HQ MELBOURNE TR.		KING ST SUPPORT
D. Coy.	B. Coy	2 guides	9.30 pm D. Coy. HQ MELBOURNE TR		QUEEN ST. RESERVE.

Secret.   7th Battalion Order No. 5.   Copy No.
              Refs. Sheets 62D 57D 1/20000

1. 7th. Bn. will be relieved by 9th. Bn. in the right sub-sector of the Bde. front on the night 27/28 in accordance with attached schedule.

2. Guides for the in-coming Bn. will report to 2/Lt. R.L. Read at Bn H.Q at 3.0 am 27th, in order to reconnoitre route. Those of A & B Coy. will return to their Coys. after reconnaissance is completed and will report again at Bn. H.Q. at 8.30 pm. Those of C & D will remain at Battn. H.Q.

3. All trench stores will be handed over including tools and food containers. Petrol Cans with the exception of Reserve of 30 per Coy. will be brought out and dumped at Bn H.Q dump by 9.30 p.m. T.O. will arrange to collect these with Sig. Stores and Medical Panniers etc. Trenches etc. will be left in a clean & sanitary condition.

4. L. Gun. limbers will report to H.Q and boy respective Coy ration dumps at 10 p.m for conveyance of guns to Henencourt Wood.

5. On completion of relief platoons will move independently to new quarters in Divnl. Res. (HENENCOURT WOOD V26a 5.9)

6. Advance parties consisting of Major C de L. Armitage and the 5 C.Q.M.S's will report to HQ 10th. Bn. Henencourt Wood at 10 am 27th. All defence schemes etc. will be ~~handed~~ taken over and arrangements will be made for accommodation of H.Q. and Coys, for the taking over of stores and for the provision of guides for the Bn. moving in when relieved.

7. Code word for relief complete "Orders carried out" Coys. will report by runner to new HQ their arrival at Henencourt Wood

8. Receipts for stores taken over and handed over will be sent to B.O.R by 12 noon the 28th.

9. Acknowledge
Distribution Normal

Sd K.O. Peppiatt
Capt. & a/Adjt.

              Schedule

7th Bn	9th Bn	Guides	Time	Place	Remarks
'A'	'C'	1 per platoon	9.30 pm	V22c88	Right Front Coy
'B'	'A'	do	do	do	Left Front Coy
'C'	'D'	do	do	do	Support Coy
'D'	'B'	do	do	do	Reserve Coy
H.Q.	H.Q.	2 guides	do	do	Murray Trench

Coys to move in order named above.

SECRET.
31-5-18

1/Battalion Order No 6
Feb 62 Dn.n 1/20,000   Copy No. 6

1. 7th Bn London Regt will be relieved by 2nd Bedo Regt today commencing at 4.30 p.m.

2. On relief Coy will move independently to their new positions on the BASIEUX System V25c (Battn HQ C6c2.2.). Five minutes interval will be allowed between platoons.

3. Coy Cmdrs will reconnoitre their new positions this morning and will send the necessary advance parties to take over stores from 7/L. Buffs. and arrange accommodation.

4. Trans B.O.R. horses together with Offrs Valises will be dumped at B.O.R by 4.30 pm.

5. T.O will arrange to convey them to the new area.

6. Receipts for stores and Ammunition taken over and handed over will be sent to B.O.R. by 9 a.m 1st June.

7. Relief complete and arrival in new positions will be notified to this office.

Distribution Normal.

Signed. Lt. W. Pepyatt
Capt. & a/Adjt.

Army Form C. 2118.

7th Kensington
Vol: 18.
June 1918

WAR DIARY
or
INTELLIGENCE SUMMARY.
(Erase heading not required.)

Instructions regarding War Diaries and Intelligence Summaries are contained in F. S. Regs., Part II. and the Staff Manual respectively. Title pages will be prepared in manuscript.

Place	Date	Hour	Summary of Events and Information	Remarks and references to Appendices
BAIZIEUX	1-6-18		Relieving 7th Buffs in BAIZIEUX SYSTEM. Reliefs taken complete 7.30pm	
	2-6-18	9/11AM	Batt. drill in Tally C Sqn. 9.30AM to 10AM. Bath in the Country. Attack practice 10-to 11 AM	
		6-to 7 PM	Company training. 11-to 3 PM Check practice. The following Officer joined for duty Lieut B S Scott. Lieut G Stanfield report to Bde to report to Mess H S Haughland, Lieut G Moats	
	3-6-18	9/11AM	Training as for 2/6/18. Gas Chamber today for 50 Shanks. Tasting classes under R.E. instructors	
	4-6-18		Station Training	
DAILY MAIL WOODS	5-6-18		Battalion moved to T.29. (DAILY MAIL WOODS) on lorries. In camp 6.30 PM	
	6-6-18	9/11/1 AM	Battn. Training - 5.30pm to 9.30pm Work on transport lines in Company training	
	7-6-18	"	" 8.30pm to 6.30pm Battn. route march to TUBERMPRE Kensington in an attack	
	8-6-18	9-15AM	In wood in T 30.6 Battalion Parade, for march past Corps Commander.	
	9-6-18	9-0?	" " " for practice counter attack	
PICQUIGNY	10-6-18	9-11	Battn moved by bus from DAILY MAIL WOODS to PICQUIGNY on Bus H - 30 PM	
	11-6-18	9-12 noon	Batt. Parade. Batt drill	
	12-6-18	9-12 noon	Three Companies Battn drill one Company firing on range	
	13-6-18	9-12	Batt. Parade for Squad attack practice. The following Officer joined for duty Lt & MG Vipond. 2/Lt Roberts	
	14-6-18	9-12	Attack practice at FOUDRINOY - Battn on sports during afternoon	
	15-6-18		Church Parade. Brig General to G Burgess D.S.O. addressed the Battalion	
BAIZIEUX	17-6-18	5.35AM	Battalion moved by bus to BAIZIEUX SYSTEM, relieving 17 TRANVILLERS - CONTAY road. relief complete 12 noon	
	18-6-18		30 Men relieving 17 R. Inskn. Fusls. reliefs complete 12.30 pm	
	19-6-18		In line	

WAR DIARY or INTELLIGENCE SUMMARY

Army Form C. 2118.

7 London Regt

June 18

Place	Date	Hour	Summary of Events and Information	Remarks and references to Appendices
IN LINE	20.6.18		On line.	
	21.6.18		"	
	22.6.18		"	
	23.6.18		"	
	24.6.18		Night 24/25, relieved by 10th Batt. 7th London Regiment. Total casualties officers nil O.R. 2 Scott	
	25.6.18		Lieut. E. Walter wounded. Organise D of R. 1 wounded 2.	
	26.6.18		Refitting - reorganization	
	27.6.18		Two Companies proceeded to R. LAVIEVILLE line taking over half the front held by 6th London	
	28.6.18		Battalion on working parties in LAVIEVILLE LINE	
	29.6.18		Two Companies in BAIZIEUX SYSTEM. Company training	
	30.6.18		Voluntary Church Service	

W Mennell
Capt. + a/Adjt
7th Battn. The London Regt.

WAR DIARY or INTELLIGENCE SUMMARY

Army Form C. 2118.

1/7 London R[egiment]
July 1918
Vol 19

Place	Date	Hour	Summary of Events and Information	Remarks and references to Appendices
BAIZIEUX	1·7·18		Other Companies in LAVIEVILLE LINE in BAIZIEUX SYSTEM	
ALBERT	2/3/18	12.30 am	Relieved 23rd London Regiment in the Left Subsector of the Divisional Front.	
	3/7/18		On the line	
	4/7/18		"	
	5/6/7/18	10.30 pm	Relieved by 2/4 London Regt. Battn. moved into Support	
	6/7/18		On Support	
	7/7/18		"	
	8/7/18		"	
	9/7/18		"	
	9/10/7/18		Relieved 6th Battalion 'Other London Regiment' in Right Sector of Left Sub-sector on the line	
	10·7·18		"	
	11·7·18		"	
	12·7·18		Other ranks casualties for Above Officers:- 2/Lt H Oberstein Wounded Remnant Hourd killed 6	
	13·7·18		Wounded 13. Relieved by 9th Battn. 'The London Regiment' Battalion in Reserve in BAIZIEUX System	
BAIZIEUX	13/14		in LAVIEVILLE LINE. 2 Companies in BAIZIEUX SYSTEM. Battalions in refitting. Lt Col A A Fonblanque D.S.O. M.C. proceeded to England	
	15/7/18		Reorganisation or refitting	
	16/7/18		Companies in LAVIEVILLE LINE 2 " in BAIZIEUX System	

WAR DIARY
or
INTELLIGENCE SUMMARY.

(Erase heading not required.) July 1917

Place	Date	Hour	Summary of Events and Information	Remarks and references to Appendices
BAIZIEUX	14/7/17		2 Companies to LAVIEVILLE LINE – 3 Companies BAIZIEUX SYSTEM	
	18/19th		— ditto —	
AUBERT			Relieved 13rd Battalion 9th London Regt. in the sector Light Brigade - AUBERT Front On Line 3rd Battn 132 High 13th Coy Pioneers Bessaco attached for instructions for 48 hours	
	20th		"	
	21 St		"	
	22nd		Total Casualties: 1 Officer killed	
	23rd		6 O.R.s wounded	
	24th		10 O.Ranks killed	
	25th		27 " wounded	
	26th			
	24/27		Battn were stopped taking over portion of front line occupied by 110th Battn later Regt. in line	
	27.		Battn relieved by 2nd Battalion 132 American Regt. and withdrew to Support	
	27/28		In Support	
	28.		"	
	29.		"	
	30		Relieved by 12th London Regt. Battn withdrew to Round Wood Camp	
ROUND CAMP WOOD	30/31		Reorganisation and refitting. Lt Col C.S. Johnson M.C. took over Command of Battalion	
	31			7th Battn, 9th London Regt.

Army Form C. 2118.

WAR DIARY
or
INTELLIGENCE SUMMARY.
(Erase heading not required.)

Instructions regarding War Diaries and Intelligence Summaries are contained in F. S. Regs., Part II. and the Staff Manual respectively. Title pages will be prepared in manuscript.

14 17/58   7 London   August 1918   20

Place	Date	Hour	Summary of Events and Information	Remarks and references to Appendices
ROUND WOOD	1.8.18.		Out on Range Inspection by C.O. Lieut Gaul to be 6° Column & to 6 crowned Command	OO114
"	2.8.18		Moved by Bus to HALLOY — Lieut PERNOIS took over Rifles 2-30 pm	
HALLOY	3.8.18		Squad and Coy Bomb Drill, Lewis Gun, Signalling, and Stretcher Bearer Classes	
"	4.8.18		Divn closing by 12 hrs. Move vice to mov's. Moved by Bus and Horse Transt to BONNAY in Position # 3cAm 5.8.15	SPORH
BONNAY IN LINE	5.8.18		Reinforced & relieve the 11th Battalion, 1st Division 12th Division in reserve on Reserve	OORS
"	6.8.18			
"	7.8.18		See Narrative attached	
"	8.8.18			
"	9.8.18			
"	10.8.18			
BRAY–CORBIE ROAD	11.8.18		Relieved in reserve near CEMETARY COPSE	
"	12.8.18		Battalion moved back to ROUND WOOD arrived at Ars at 7-30 pm	
ROUND WOOD	13.8.18		Cleaning and Refitting — Lewis Guns and Rifle Inspection by Armourer Sgt.	
"	14.8.18		Battalion drawing Lewis Guns on Charge — reinforcements joined as follows 2nd Lieuts	
"	15.8.18		J. Davidson, E.J. Hooper, 61 textils, W.H. Davidson, C.D. @ Case fam, C.D. Kenneth	
"	16.8.18		J. Danton — lift scott, Of & Fraser, J.E. Emily, OS light fresh, and 293 Other Ranks (Detailed form Officers and Sections, Number and Battalion pages)	

Army Form C. 2118.

WAR DIARY
or
INTELLIGENCE SUMMARY.
(Erase heading not required.)

of ....8 August 1918........

Instructions regarding War Diaries and Intelligence Summaries are contained in F. S. Regs., Part II. and the Staff Manual respectively. Title pages will be prepared in manuscript.

Place	Date	Hour	Summary of Events and Information	Remarks and references to Appendices
ROUND WOOD	16.8.18		Nº 3 under Company Commanders – All Junior Officers under 2.i.c. from 9AM to 10 AM. Non-Coms instructed by Medical Officer. Baths allotted from 5 PM to 8 PM. Batts allotted from 9AM to 12.30PM afternoon Remainder of day baths or Battalion in Extends from	
"	17.8.18		Army Ludus. Niagara. Church Services	
"	18.8.18		9AM to 10AM A.G.D (parade under Company Commanders) B Company firing on 30 yards Range. 10.15AM to 12.30 PM Battalion training.	
"	19.8.18		9AM to 10AM A.B.C.D bays under Company Commanders. 10 AM to 12 noon Platoon & Coy drill 12 noon to 12.30pm Bath drill	
"	20.8.18		Companies at disposal of Company Commanders 9AM to 11AM. 11AM to 1 PM Platoon practice attacks.	
"	21.8.18		Battalion moved to position near HELLY to point ½ ALBERT – AMIENS road 1 W of MORLANCOURT	
	22.8.18		See Narrative attached	
	23.8.18			
	24.8.18			
	25.			
	26.8			
	27.8/18			
	28.			

W P Kennard
Lieut & Adjutant
7th Bn London Regt

174th Bde.

58th Div.

7th BATTALION

LONDON REGIMENT

AUGUST 1918

7th. Battn. The London Regiment.

Narrative of Operations 8th. 9th. and 10th. August, 1918.

Reference sheet 62D NE 1/20000

1. Approach March and Assembly.

At 10.20 p.m. on the 7th. the Bn. moved forward from Valley in J22c. along the line of BEGA trench - COOTAMUNDRA street and CRUMP lane to their assembly position in k.25.a. The Coy. were disposed as follows:- "D" Coy. on right then 2 coys of the 6th. Lon. Rgt. on a one Coy. front then "B" Coy. with "A" Coy on left: "C" Coy in support behind "A" and "B" Coys. Front Line Coys. occupied a front of 120 yards each and were formed in two waves of small columns with a skirmishing line in front; Support Coy. was 250 yds. behind the leading Coy. in line of half platoons in file.

On the right flank of the Bn. were the two remaining Coys. of 6th. Bn. with 8th. Bn. in Reserve behind them. The left flank of the Bn. rested on Crump Lane at K.25.a.7.7. with 36th. Inf.Bde. on left to North of CRUMP lane. Bn. H.Q. was at LONE TREE CEMETERY J.24.6.2.

Assembly was retarded by the fact that the 173rd. Inf. Bde. and 36th. Inf. Bde. were using the same approach route at the same time.

There was little counter prepartion by the enemy and although it appeared later from prisoners statements that he was expecting a a local attack the actual time and scope of it were a surprise.

Shortly before 4 a.m. on the 8th. a heavy mist fell and by Zero hour (4.20 a.m.) it was impossible to see more then 20 to 25 yds.

The tanks which were cooperating on the Bn. front were late and only passed Bn. H.Q. at 4.18 a.m.

173rd. Inf. Bde. were assembled in rear of my assembly position.

2. OBJECTIVES.

The ultimate objective of the Bn. was the line K.27.d.9.4. - K27.b.9.7. "A" and "B" Coys. passing round to the N side of MALARD Wood supported by "C" Coy. and "D" Coy. containing the N.W. side of the Wood from k.26.d.9.5. to K.27.d.65.95.
173rd. Inf. Bde. were to pass through one hour later and take a further line beyond on the SOMME RIVER.

3. THE ASSAULT.

The barrage opende punctually at 4.20 a.m. and was very good. Troops at once advanced to the assault in the heavy mist which made direction very difficult and without the tanks which had not yet arrived. owing to the mist it was impossible to observe the progress of the operation but batches of wounded and prisoners soon began to arrive and as information filtered back I gathered that progress was satisfactory at any rate as far as MALARD Wood. I then moved my H.Q. forward to a small Quarry to K.26.B.0.8. and went forward with my Adjt.to ascertain the position. The mist was now beginning to clear and the enemy shelling which had been considerable to start with was diminishing. I made my way to MALARD Wood and found the nucleus of my Bn. at the Ravine in K.27.a and b. under Capt. P. Halley-Jones.

Situation was then as follows:- In the heavy mist touch and direction were inevitable lost, the situation E of MALARD Wood was not known and my left flank was in the air. the 173rd. Inf. Bde. had become scattered in the fog and had not carried out their role. I then reorganised my Bn. and pushed them forward to the high ground in K.27.b. with orders to push out to both flanks to gain touch. At that time there were 3 Officers and 77 other ranks present. I kept in my own hand some elements of the 8th. Bn. who reported to me and also some of the 6th. Bn. Elements of the 173rd. Inf. Bde. were also filtering up: these I had organised and posted them on my left flank at K.27.a.9.9.

"A" Coy. of the Suffolk pioneers were meanwhile digging to form a flank in K.26.b.

The situation on both flanks was still obscure,

and there appeared to be enemy machine guns firing from about K.33 central. I then found two Coy. of the 2/2nd. London Regt. advancing in K26.c. and finding that they had no definite instructions, I arranged with the senior Coy. Commander to deploy and advance through MALARD Wood. I got them the assistance of a Tank and of 174th. L.T.M.B. This movement was carried out without opposition and they advanced to the East side of the Wood.

I then returned to my Bn. and found they had got touch with a party of the 6th. Londons digging in near the Quarry at K.27.d.9.0

By this time our line was established from K.27.d.4.9. to K.27.b.3.7. with Lewis Gun Posts pushed out in front, but it was not till the afternoon that the situation on my left was finally cleared up by the 5th. Royal Berks establishing a line from K.27.b.2.9. to K.21.a.3.7. I then sent away all troops with me of other Regts. except 3 Officers 60 men 8th. London Regt. whom I kept in the Ravine in K.27.a. and b. as a counter attack force.

4. FURTHER OPERATIONS.

On the evening of the 8th. an abortive attack was launched by 173rd. Inf. Bde. on my right flank and subsequently the 9th. London Regt. took over the line E of MALARD Wood leaving elements of the 173rd. Inf. Bde. in between my right and left flank.

On the afternoon of the 9th. the Troops of the 8th. London Regt. with me were withdrawn as further operations were contemplated. By that time I had collected scattered elements of my own Bn. and had at my disposal 6 Coy. Officers and about 200 other ranks.

I had no precise instructions as to the operation but I understood the American Troops were to attack GRESSAIRE WOOD from my left flank at 5.30 p.m. and that I had to advance on their right to the River SOMME at K.29 central. I had barely time to instruct my officers as to their role and objectives. I put my main force under Capt. P. Halley-Jones and detached a platoon to advance on my right as I feared machine gun nests on my right and was uninformed as to what troops were operating there. I had with me my Adjutant and Capt. G.G. JACKSON: my H.Q. were in the ravine at K.27.a.8.5.

5. SECOND ASSAULT.

At 5.30 p.m. on the 9th. the barrage opened. The American Troops not assembled in time to take full advantage of it but tanks went forward and assisted in breaking down opposition. My own force being already in position on the high ground got away ahead of the American Troops and encountered severe machine gun fire but advanced steadily, gallantly led by Capt. Halley Jones who unluckily was not long after mortally wounded.

After passing the high ground and reaching the edge of the wood in K28. central the opposition was less but casualties in officers were very heavy and the survivors of the assaulting troops reached K.29.a.1.0 without Officers. I received information of this situation and I sent forward Capt. G.G. Jackson to take charge and he carried them on to the top of the ridge at K.29.d.5.7. Instructions had been so lacking that none of the men knew where there objective was.

At 6.20 p.m. I and my Adjt. with H.Q. Lewis Guns moved forward and from K.27.b.9.6. I was able to observe British and American troops establishing posts on the ridge S.E. but fighting still appeared to be going on to my right in the lower ground and also in GRESSAIRE Wood. I pushed forward picking up some stragglers on the way and finally had 35 other ranks and 5 Lewis Guns with me when I joined Capt JACKSON who had only 30 other ranks with him whom he was establishing in posts on the ridge. There were American Troops on my right and left - 4 Coys of my right and one on my left. I also took charge of about 20 other ranks of the 12th. London Regt. who had arrived there. All opposition had now died down with the exception of two machine guns on the ridge at K.29.b.1.9. I sent Capt. G.G. JACKSON back as he was wounded.

3.

With my own men and those of the 12th. London Regt. I established a line from K.29.a.8.3. to K.29.c.5.4. I arranged with the American Coy. on my left for them to deal with the two machine guns above mentioned and to establish a line of posts to get touch with troops on their left flank which was in the air, The American Troops on my right undertook the picketing of the bridge river crossing at K.29.d.3.3.

My Adjutant Capt. K.O. PEPPIATT, did invaluable work in assembling the Americans on my left to organise their defences and he personally led parties of them to drive off the machine guns at K.29.b.1.9. and captured 11 prisoners.

Touch on my left in GRESSAIRE WOOD was still lacking, so I arranged with the American Officer in charge on my right to move two of his companies up through GRESSAIRE WOOD to fill in the gap which he accordingly did at 5 a.m. on 16th. and the line was then finally established. I then reported the situation personally to Bde. H.Q.

On the night 10th. after there had been considerable fighting north of GRESSAIRE WOOD during the afternoon, the Bn. was relieved by American Troops and moved back to MALARD WOOD.

6. GENERAL.

(a) In both assaults numerous T.M.S., Heavy and light machine guns were captured and many prisoners. In each case the severest fighting and the most prisoners were in the enemy's front line. In the second assault 4 field guns and 3 5.9 howitzers were captured the latter in GRESSAIRE WOOD, K.28.b.9.3. and the former K.28.a.9.3. and K.28.d.9.5. A wagon of signalling stores was also captured at K.29.a.3.4.
The heavy mist undoubtably helped in assaulting the enemy forward defence on the 8th. inst. that was largely responsible for the failure of the second phase.

(b) Communication was lacking to strart with owing to the failure of the Bde. Signallers to establish exchanges in accordance to plan. On 8th. inst. my Bn. established communication by wire at 10.30 a.m. from K.26.c.1.9. back to LONE TREE CEMY. at 2 p.m. by lamp from K.26.b.8.2. to K.26.c.1.9. By 4 p.m. the line was run out to K.26.b.8.2. and was maintained throughout. Two lines were laid into the ravine at K.27.a.8.5. but it was found impossible to maintain them owing to shell fire. The wire for these lines was collected by my signallers on the ground as their own supply was inadequate.

(c) Medical Arrangements. On the 9th. inst the supply of stretchers was wholly inadequate and supplies demanded were very slow in arriving. Many wounded lying out in front at no great distance from the R.A.P. could not have been collected much earlier, were it possible to supply R.A.M.C. Bearers on this work. At present M.O!s are forbidden to use them forward of the R.A.P. even when things are quiet.

(d) H.Q. Lewis Guns proved extremely useful in furninshing an intact and fresh reserve to be brought forward after the objectiv had been taken. I recommend that each Bn. be supplied with a light German machine gun for instructional purposes as a knowledg of their use would be very useful to assaulting troops.

(e) Supply Tanks fulfilled their role well. I recommend that a Q.M.Sgt. travel with them to remain in charge of the dump when formed and to ensure the supplies reaching the troops for whom they are intended. The Bn. received some S.A.A. from 'plane.

(f) Casualties were unfortunately heavy on both days amounting to 12 officers and about 300 other Ranks.

In conclusion I would bring to notice the gallant services and excellent work done by the following officers:-

4.

Capt. P. HALLEY-JONES, M.C. (Died of Wounds).

Capt. K.O. PEPPIATT.

2nd. Lieut. A.C. FRASER.

2nd. Lieut. E.W. PINNOCK.

                              Lieut. Colonel.
                    Commanding 7th. Battalion,
                            The London Regiment.

7th. Battalion, The London Regiment.

Narrative of Operations August 25th. to September 1st. 1918.

Reference 62D NE and 62C NW
1/20,000

25th.   At 1.30 a.m. on 25/8/18 the Battalion moved forward from a position S.W. of MORLANCOURT to the N end of the BOIS DES TAILLES, whence they again moved forward at 8 a.m. to a position of readiness E of the HAPPY VALLEY.
At 7 p.m. the Battn. assembled on the E slope of the valley in L4 and F32 (with 6th. Battn. in support behind right flank and 8th. Battn. in support behind left flank) preparatory to an advance to take over and establish a line E of BILLON WOOD gained by elements of the 173rd. Bde.
Owing to difficulties in getting touch with the Australians on the right, who were to cooperate, the advance was delayed and was finally begun at 10.15 p.m.
A violent thunderstorm made progress slow, as the darkness and blinding rain made it difficult to keep touch and direction but the line E of BILLON WOOD was established successfully and touch gained with the Australians on the right at COPSE H (A26cD) and the elements of 173rd. Brigade were relieved. Battn. H.Q. was established at TRIGGER WOOD.

26th.   The intention was for the Battn. to push forward patrols during the night of 25/26th. and gain 1500 yards of ground up to a barrage line W of CREST AVENUE (A28a) and trench in A22c and a. The late receipt of orders and the late hour at which it was possible to organize E of BILLON WOOD. made it impossible to push forward till 4.10 a.m. on 26th. The barrage opened on above line at 4 a.m. and lifted forward at 4.30 a.m. till it reached the intended final objective of the old British Front Line in A23a and c.
       The 7th. Battn. covered the whole Brigade front with the 8th. Bn. in close support and the 6th. Bn. in reserve. The 1500 yards from the start line and the barrage line was open ground covered by hostile machine gun fire and considerable opposition was encountered. With no barrage protection progress was slow and difficult and casualties rather heavy. Owing to a mistake the Australians on our right did not advance though the 173rd. Brigade advanced on our left.
       In the event this Bn. reached a position in A27a just W of D Copse and along the contour towards C Copse and could progress no further, the slope in front of them and to the flanks being stiff with machine guns and their right flank in the air. Casualties were severe on the left flank but the elements who reached D Copse managed to maintain themselves there for 8 hours under continuous machine gun fire and beat off attempts to envelop their flanks by enemy machine guns creeping round. It was a fine piece of work. The Officers in Command were Capt. J.H.JACKSON "B" Coy. and 2nd. Lt. L.H.WALSH M.C.,D.C.M. "D" Coy.
       Meanwhile 173rd. Bde. elements were reported in C Copse, which is not visible from D Copse but communication between the two was impossible and communication to the rear was hazardous.
       The 8th. Bn. were established in front of and N of BILLON WOOD and 2 platoons of 7th. Bn. were between BILLON WOOD and H Copse. The 6th. Bn. were in reserve at TRIGGER WOOD.

2.

By the afternoon Australian Troops had worked forward on our right and finally got touch with 7th.Bn. at D Copse. The resolution of this party in maintaining their position was of the highest value to the Australians and acted as a pivot on which they swung round and advanced northward to close up the line between MARICOURT Valley and the River SOMME. Had this party been driven back the whole advance would have been delayed.

Two Field Guns were captured by 7th. Bn. at A27a2.5.

Company Commanders:- "A" Capt J.G.H. Budd, "B" Capt J.H. Jackson "C" Lieut F.E. Moylan, "D" Lieut L.H. Walsh M.C. D.C.M.

27th. At 4.55 a.m. on 27/8/18 the operation was continued; 7th.Bn. on right, 6th. on the left and 8th. Bn. in support. Australians on right flank and 173rd. Bde. on left flank.

Bde. objective was the old British Front Line in A29a and A23c and a, with an exploitation line on the old German Reserve Line in A30a and A24c and a.

Coy. 8th. Bn. was in close support of 7th. Bn, with orders to clear FARGNY WOOD and take the objective in A29a. Each front Bn. had one section M.G.s. of "B" Coy, M.G.Bn. attached to them and 2 sections were in reserve.

The Bn. assembled E of D Copse and worked forward to the barrage which lifted in six minutes. The usual resistance by machine gun nests was encountered and overcome but not without casualties.

At 7.25 a.m. Bn. H.Q. was moved forward to the Quarry in A28a: the situation in front was still obscure but prisoners were coming in and ultimately it was ascertained that 6th. and 7th. Bn. had reached the old British Front Line and after reorganization a line was firmly established there. Further exploitation was not attempted as the ridges ahead were firmly held.

7th. Bn. captured one Field Gun at A23c7.7.

On night 27/28th. the 8th.Bn. came in on the right relieving 7th. Bn. who reorganized in Road Avenue and then **28th.** pushed forward again to take up a defensive position in old British line in support of the further attack which was launched from there at 4.55 a.m. on 28/8/18 by 8th. and 6th. Bns. Objective old German Reserve line with exploitation line in B25a, B19c and 19a.

The objective was gained and finally posts established in front but not without opposition. 7th. Bn. suffered casualties from enemy counter barrage.

At night the Brigade was relieved by 10th. and 12th. **29th.** Bns. the London Regiment, 175th. Brigade and 7th. Bn. reached its bivouac area at B Copse, S.W. of MARICOURT, on morning of 29/8/18.

During this period the Bn. suffered casualties of 13 Officers and 280 Other Ranks.
The Officers were:-
Killed on 26th. 2nd.Lt. C.L.MOORE
   "   "   27th. 2nd.Lt. J.E.TROLLIP.
   "   "   "   2nd. Lt V.A.TYLER
   "   "   "   2nd.Lt. E.H.J.MAULE-FFINCH.
Missing on 26th Lieut. F.E.MOYLAN.
   "   "   "   2nd.Lt. H.COCKROFT.
Wounded on 26th 2nd.Lt. J.L.SYDENHAM.
   "   "   27th 2nd.Lt. W.H.STOCKER
   "   "   26th 2nd.Lt. W.H.B.DAVIDSON.
   "   "   26th 2nd.Lt. J.C.HARTLEY
   "   "   27th Captain J.G.H.BUDD
   "   "   27th 2nd.Lt. L.H.WALSH......,D.C.M.
                         (Died of Wounds 29/8/18.)
   "   "   29th Major R.J.A.HENNIKER. M.C.
             (attached 8th.Bn. Temporarily)

3.

On evening of 30th. inst. the Bn. embussed at MARICOURT and proceeded along the PERONNE road debussing at HEM WOOD whence they marched to concentration point at JUNCTION WOOD (B28b).

31st.
At 2 a.m. orders were received that the Brigade would attack MARRIERES WOOD (C13 and 19) under a barrage starting at 5.10 a.m. and lifting forward at 5.30 a.m. 6th. Bn. on the right and 8th. Bn. on left, 7th. Bn. in support.

At 3.30 a.m. the Bn. moved from JUNCTION WOOD to their assembly position in B26d and were placed in position by the Adjutant Capt. K.O.PEPPIATT. "C" and "D" Coys. leading Coys., "A" and "B" Coys in support. Their orders were not to enter MARRIERES WOOD till it had been cleared by the assaulting Bns. or unless assistance was necessary and in any event "A" and "B" Coys. were to remain in Brigade Reserve west of the Wood, but there had been no time to explain orders fully and when the assault took place, No. 9 and 10 Platoons under 2nd.Lt. COOKE followed through with the 6th. Bn., worked right through the wood and across the valley in C20d and along the far slope to the OLD QUARRY in C20b cutting off a number of enemy who were retiring down the eastern slope of MARRIERES WOOD and making them prisoners.

They established themselves in the OLD QUARRY with elements of the 6th. and 8th. Bns.: this was 500 yards beyond the objective laid down and its capture and retention was of the greatest assistance in securing the left flank of the Australian Troops operating on our right and assuring the position was E of MARRIERES WOOD.

Later on "D" Coy. and the remainder of "C" Coy. who had remained on the West side of the Wood were pushed forward. "C" Coy. joined 9 and 10 Platoons in the OLD QUARRY C20b and "D" Coy. established themselves in the other OLD QUARRY, C20d. The 6th. Bn. were in between these two Coys.: elements of the 8th. Bn. were with "C" Coy.7th.Bn. and in touch with the Australians. Remainder of 8th.Bn. were on ridge E of the Wood opposite the village of BOUCHAVESNES.

"A" and "B" Coys. 7th.Bn. moved to C19a central in MARRIERES WOOD. Small parties of the enemy filtered back through BOUCHAVESNES village but were held in check by Lewis Gun fire from the OLD QUARRY in C20b.

Battalion H.Q. remained throughout at JUNCTION WOOD.

Some 300 prisoners, two guns and two light mortars were taken by the Brigade; the morale of the prisoners of the 23nd. Division was low.

Casualties 3 Officers and 17 Other Ranks.

2nd.Lt. A.C.FRASER Commanding "C" Coy. was killed while stalking an enemy sniper who was causing casualties in the OLD QUARRY; Capt. K.O.PEPPIATT was wounded at duty. 2nd.Lt. HARBOTT was severely wounded with 6th.Bn.

1st.
On 1/9/18 173rd. Bde. passed through 174th. Bde. to carry on the attack.

8th. Bn. elements were withdrawn from OLD QUARRY and reorganised in MARRIERES WOOD; at night 174th. Bde. was relieved and marched back to bivouacs in B20b near BATTERY COPSE.

Lieut. Colonel.
Commanding 7th. Bn. The London Regt.

7 London R

Army Form C. 2118.
174/58

WAR DIARY
of
INTELLIGENCE SUMMARY.
(Erase heading not required.)

October 1918

Place	Date	Hour	Summary of Events and Information	Remarks and references to Appendices
HEM WOOD	1-9-18		Battalion resting in trenches near HEM WOOD	
	2-9-18		C.O.'s clothing rifle & equipment inspection	
	3-9-18		Platoon training, Lewis Gun class a.d. plan	
	4-9-18		" " " "	
	5-9-18		Platoon and company training	
			Lewis gun instruction, Bomb class, musketry training	
	6-9-18		Orders received to stand by at 7-30pm ready to move	
	7-9-18			
	8-9-18			
	9-9-18			
	10-9-18		See narrative attached	
	11-9-18			
LIERAMONT	12-9-18		Battalion withdraw to BUS at LIERAMONT	
	13-9-18		Reorganising and refitting. 2nd Lieut Lindsay	
	14-9-18		Tyler & Ready Evans transferred by Canadian Brigade to .... M.O's....	
	15-9-18		Bath visited 17 stoves by nearly 60 .... at	
			10 A.O.Battalion the London Regt	
			Marching into "A" and "C" Coys in front "B" and "D" Support	
	16-9-18			
	17-9-18		A Company withdraw to LIERAMONT at 2 A.M. 17/18	

Army Form C. 2118.

WAR DIARY
or
INTELLIGENCE SUMMARY
(Erase heading not required.)

Instructions regarding War Diaries and Intelligence Summaries are contained in F. S. Regs., Part II. and the Staff Manual respectively. Title pages will be prepared in manuscript.

Place	Date	Hour	Summary of Events and Information	Remarks and references to Appendices
LIERAMONT	18.9.18		B.G.D. Began withdrawal to billets at LIERAMONT	
	19.9.18		Reorganisation, Coy inspection	
	20.9.18		Battn. having a trek on Lewis Guns	
	21.9.18		A.M. Open order & to hours notice to move. Orders to move received from Brigade	
		10.45 P.M.	Battn moved at 8.45 p.m. to Railway Embankment East of VILLERS	
			FAUCON entraining at Stat.. "The Queens" in Tiers	
			C. Head Qrs. moved forward to TINCOURT 2-30pm	
RONSOY	22.9.18		at RONSOY	
	23.9.18			
	24.9.18		"	
	25.9.18		followed by Transport and returning to Railway Embankment East of NURLU	
	26.9.18		TINCOURT HAM 25H entrained and proceed to HEILLY arrived in billets 9-30am	
	27.9.18		Entrained at HEILLY at 2-45am and proceeded to AUBIGNY AREA arrived at	
	28.9.18		CANADA CAMP 4-35AM 31-9-18	
	29.9.18		Reorganisation & refitting	
	30.9.18		Church Parades	
			Proceeded by bus to Fosse 10 for 6 months course to Gen. B.A. Lieut.	
			C. Gibbons D Coy Reserve Batt. Hqrs. M.6.a.90-25	

W.D.Annand
Captain
7th Bn. The Gordon Highlanders
H.Q.

7th. Battalion, The London Regiment.

Narrative of Operations 6th. to 11th. September, 1918.

Reference Sheet 62C N.W. & N.E. 1/20000.

6th.   On the night 6th./7th. September, 1918, the Bn. embussed at HEM WOOD and debussed just west of MOISLAINS.

7th.   Marched to GURLU WOOD relieving the 24th. London Regt. Remained in GURLU WOOD all day.

8th.   At 12.30 a.m. marched from GURLU WOOD to assembly position in E.4.c., N of SAULCOURT preparatory to an assault on EPEHY. Battn. H.Q. at E.4.c.4.1.

Barrage line was on grid line N.& S. through E.5.central and assembly position was intended to be on line of trench running N. & S. through E5.c. which was supposed to be held by 12th. Division; their posts here however had been withdrawn to E.4.c and d. and also the intended assembly position was on a forward slope in view of the enemy. As Zero hour was 7.30 a.m. the Bn. assembled in the dead ground in E.4.c. east of the road and immediately in rear of the forward posts of the Buffs. "A"."B". and "C" Coys in front line; "D" Coy. in Support.

8th. Battn. The London Regt. were assembled on our left: 6th. Bn. in support just N of GUYENCOURT-SAULCOURT. As we were assembled 1000 yards in rear of the barrage line, skirmishing line advanced at 7.20 a.m. to gain ground up to the barrage. The assaulting Bns. moved forward at 7.30 a.m. and met with considerable opposition from machine guns, strongly posted in and around the village of EPEHY. A few prisoners of the 10th. JAEGER Bn. and 14th. JAEGER Bn. were taken by the 7th. Bn. but we were unable to progress further than the line between E.5.d. and E.6.c. Casualties had been heavy (mostly wounded) and all attempts to push further forward were crushed by heavy machine gun fire.

Meanwhile the 8th. Bn. on our left had gained considerably more ground than we had but eventually had to give it up and a line was formed in and around the trenches running through E.5.b.and d. as follows:-

    "B" Coy. in shell holes amongst wire in E.5.d.9.4.
    "C" and "D" Coys. in trenches E.5.D.5.5 to E.5.d.6.7.
        and in touch with 8th. Bn. on left.
    "A" Coy. in sunken road E.5.d.4.4.

One Coy. of 6th. Bn. (which had been sent to support our right flank and ultimately to work to the right and establish connection with 74th. Division on our right after EPEHY had been taken) was in sunken road E.5.d.3.3.

Strength of Coys. at the time about 30 average.

Movement on forward zone was difficult owing to machine gun fire but communication was maintained by runner to Bn.H.Q. and a telephone was established at E.5.d.3.3. to Bn. H.Q. at E.4.c.4.1.

At night 6th. Bn. relieved 7th. Bn. who withdrew to trenches and shelters from N.E. corner of GUYENCOURT - SAULCOURT to E.3.Central. Bn. H.Q. at E.3.c.8.5.

Casualties this day:- 4 Officers wounded.
                100 other ranks (mostly wounded)

Prisoners:- 30.

9th.   Rested till night.

At 7 p.m. received verbal orders at LIERAMONT from B.G.C. 173rd. Inf. Bde. at whose disposal 7th. Bn. had been put for following days operations, one Coy. 8th. Bn. being attached to 7th. Bn.

173rd. Bde. were to attack EPEHY, 2nd. and 4th. Bns. on left, 3rd. Bn. on right. 3rd. Bn. were to assemble in E.12.b. and attack in a north-easterly direction. Role of 7th. Bn. (plus one Coy. 8th. Bn.), to form a defensive flank in E.7.c and a.   No written operation orders reached me before the

2.

At 11.30 p.m. moved forward to road in E.4.c.3.0. to concentrate with "A" Coy. 8th. Bn. Waited there until 1.30 a.m. but "A" Coy. 8th. Bn. failed to arrive.

10th.   At 1.30 a.m. on 10th. moved off with 7th. Bn. only in driving rain and very dark night which made progress very slow and finally reached in E.18.b.6.5. at 5.5. a.m. Men wet through and very tired and rations spoilt by rain.

Coys. (organised as one Coy. under Lt. BRADFIELD) moved up road towards EPEHY and established posts at E.12.d.9.1. F.7.c.4.2., F.7.c.3.4., E.12.d.9.5., Bn. H.Q. in QUARRY E.18.c.9.8. Gained touch with 14th. BLACK WATCH on right.

Zero hour was 5.15 a.m. 3rd. London Regt. attacked and were reported by casualties to have entered EPEHY.

7th. Bn. established a post at F.7.c.0.7. but could progress no further as enemy were holding trenches in F.7.a. central and F.7.a.4.8. which had not been included in the barrage: and my orders did not include offensive action.

The 3rd. London Regt. had to withdraw from EPEHY which was reoccupied by the enemy; my patrol got touch with 3rd. Bn. at E.12.central.

Position at nightfall was 6th. and 3rd. London Regts. in road running through E.12.central. 7th. London Regt. in road from E.12.d.9.2. to F.7.c.0.7. with posts eastward.

At night 7th. Bn. withdrew to LIERAMONT on relief by "D" 11th. Coy. 1/4th. SUFFOLK PIONEERS arriving 2 a.m. 11th.

Casualties this day:- 4 Other ranks.

The number and character of the troops holding EPEHY were of a different order to those previously encountered in recent fighting. A determined and organised defence was put up by a higher class of troops, who did not make the facile surrender customary recently. Their morale and general attitude were in a much higher plane. Also the hostile artillery was stronger Our troops were tired and weak in numbers and the bulk of the Officers and men unexperienced in any form of warfare.

Lieut. Colonel.
Commanding 7th. Bn. The London Regiment.

WAR DIARY or INTELLIGENCE SUMMARY

Army Form C. 2118.

Place	Date	Hour	Summary of Events and Information	Remarks and references to Appendices
M10a R.4	1-10-18	—	Reference 1/20,000 M4 a N.W. On the night 1/2nd Oct. the Batt. took over the left sub-sector of the MAROC Section in front of LOOS, relieving 2nd Bn. Rifle Brigade. A & D Coy's in line. M & A R.4. Coy Commanders were 'A' Coy 2nd Lieut. R.H. Stanton, 'C' Coy Lieut. A.J. Mostyn, 'B' Coy 2nd Lieut. R.H. Stanton, 'D' Coy Lieut. J.B. Bradhurst. Major J.G. Hyndes D.S.O. in command of Battalion.	
	2-10-18		On dawn on 2nd Oct. the Bangers on our left reported the enemy to have evacuated his front line on their front. Patrols were sent out to ascertain if the same thing had happened on the Batt. front. They were fired at from the right flank HERMAN STOKES Sap by Germans on the main Loos ab Lens. and patrols withdrew after capturing two prisoners. Later these two platoons of "A" & "B" Coys advanced, capturing BOISDINHUIT in which 1 Officer + 14 Other Ranks were taken prisoner, and advanced to HALIBUT trench where they were joined by the rest of 'A' & 'B' Coys. B.H.Q. moved into the approach to HYTHE TUNNEL (H32d.4.4). Oct. 12th having 2 further advance was made under cover of bombardment of the BURGAN Tunnel and the Railway on H34 H.Q. and afterwards considerable resistance at MORTAR WOOD had been established. Advance on the Railway in H34 b & d.	
HYTHE TUNNEL	3-10-18		At dawn on the 3rd Oct. the BURGAN Tunnel was again bombarded by our artillery and in advance of which A & B Coys advanced and took the Railway in H35 a, b, d, and H29 d. Further advance was impossible. ENEMY wire along Railway wire not cut.	
HALIBUT TRENCH A31.a.4.6			B.H.Q. moved to HALIBUT TRENCH H34.a.4.6. No further advance was made during day.	

Army Form C. 2118.

WAR DIARY
or
INTELLIGENCE SUMMARY.
(Erase heading not required.)

Instructions regarding War Diaries and Intelligence Summaries are contained in F. S. Regs., Part II. and the Staff Manual respectively. Title pages will be prepared in manuscript.

Place	Date	Hour	Summary of Events and Information	Remarks and references to Appendices
HALIBUT TRENCH H.31.a.1.4.	4-10-18		Batn held the line of the Railway in H.37 + H.3 & H.31 and H.31.d. during the relief during the night & dawn, and until the early morning the dawn towards line ANTRY–MUNTBY trench which would be strongly occupied each day	
	5-10-18		Batn was disposed on Capt A. 2 Coys on the front line (C & D) & A Coy in support	
	6-10-18		"B" Coy on Range at HALIBUT TRENCH. Capt F.B. Forrest left the line wounded yet due and went on leave 6th Oct. 2nd & 3rd Lts assuming duty of the same. 2Lt. R.A. Ruson held in a bombed on 6th with 2Lt & Bn.	
	7-10-18		assuming command of B Coy	
	8-10-18		Batn was relieved by the 10th Bath and moved to Billets in LIEVIN	
	8/9-10-18		Batn was resting at LIEVIN	
	10-10-18		On 1st Oct, 2Lt. S.H. Vaughan joined the Batn and assumed command of B Coy	
	11-10-18		Ref 1/20,000 44a Sht.	
LIÉVIN	12-10-18	14.15	Batn was ordered to move at 14.15 to billets in vicinity of SALLAUMINES. Batn moved off at 14.15 and on arrival at SALLAUMINES, at the R.R. 400—, had not arrived owing to a breakdown of busses was ordered to proceed to the new guide was at COURRIÈRES and take over from 10th Queens 18th Div. Sector.	
		18.30	The Batn moved off from SALLAUMINES at 18.30 and arrived at H.Q. Queens at 015.c.8.9 at 20.30 after delay being caused by negotiations of Bath in turning a road leading to be found round, the backs of houses in a very dark night. Coys of Bn then moved in to the left sector of the 18th Div Front were conducted by guides, "B" being the last Coy under Relay line Coys "B" Coy line centre "C" Coy left, right. "B" Coy found 2 subs. 1 Lys CORONS.	

B.H.Q. 015.c.8.0

Army Form C. 2118.

WAR DIARY
or
INTELLIGENCE SUMMARY.
(Erase heading not required.)

Instructions regarding War Diaries and Intelligence Summaries are contained in F. S. Regs., Part II. and the Staff Manual respectively. Title pages will be prepared in manuscript.

Place	Date	Hour	Summary of Events and Information	Remarks and references to Appendices
O.15.d.8.9	12-10-18		Reinforcements arrived last night in lorries. 2 coys from front at Somerill S & D. 50 o.r. from B.H. 1/140,000 Hill 2.	
O.16.d.8.9	13-10-18	05.30	Bourn pushed out strong points at Journils cam brick with the enemy between Sources road and SURRIERE. Bn, in touch with the Bucks and Sussex who by strong covers SURRIERE had scylant was still in resistance. 'A' 'B' Coys were feed by the Bn from MARAIS WOOD and trenches 1000 yds E of COURRIERES. 'C' Coy advanced about 600 yds on the right but were held up by the same recon.	
	13/14-10-18		Bn support line was formed on Eastern outskirts of COURRIERES in which truth was reinforced by 8th Batts. and westernmost trenches. 'B' 'C' 'D' Coys in MONTIGNY trench and FOLIE trenches. 'A' Coy in support on the Old MONTIGNY tram line.	
	14-10-18		Bn reformed in Bde Reserve, to role being detailed to the MONTIGNY trench in Z Row and counter attack Shelton Avon. Runners were A/Coy 2 Lt ? W. Simpson M.C., 'B' Coy 2 Lt Woolner 'C' Coy Lieut. O.B. Mahaes, 'D' Coy Lieut. J.W.M. Shape Lt. Col. L.G. Shelton D.S.O., M.C., in command of Batt.	
			2nd Lt. Ld. Pinnock M.C. left for Rest Camp. One Lt. & 24 troops assuming command Bn - 103 Reinforcements arrived as follows 5 other Ranks	
	15-10-18	05.30	P.L. water advanced at dawn to the canal and secured the crossings at J.25d.	
		14.00	Ok 14.00 'D' Coy was ordered up to form a defensive flank on the march along HAITE-DEULE canal - MARAIS WOOD 2 J.25 as Bn was on our left had not advanced level with us and placed in support of Bn Hqrs. for this purpose. Remaining 3 Coys took up outpost position E of COURRIERES evacuated by the 8th South lnf. Bn. H.Q. having to COURRIERES B.Y.C. Coys ('B' on right, 'C' on left) moved to West bank of canal on J.25 & 31 N.Y.S of OIGNIES -	
COURRIERES		22.00	COURRIERES road with a view to forcing through the 8th Batln. on the following morning Reinforcements arrived as follows - 3 other ranks	

D.D. & L., London, E.C.
(A10266) Wt W 5300/P713 750,000 2/18 Sch. 52 Forms/C2118/16

Army Form C. 2118.

WAR DIARY
or
INTELLIGENCE SUMMARY.
(Erase heading not required.)

Instructions regarding War Diaries and Intelligence Summaries are contained in F. S. Regs., Part II. and the Staff Manual respectively. Title pages will be prepared in manuscript.

Place	Date	Hour	Summary of Events and Information	Remarks and references to Appendices
COURRIERES	10-10-18	05:30	Strong patrols were pushed out by 'B' & 'C' Coys and followed up by three Coys, OIGNIES being taken by the midday. 'D' Coy was meanwhile relieved by 'A' Coy 6th Batn. and joined A. Coy in support on E bank of HAUTE-DEULE CANAL at J.25.d.1.4.	SS5/
J25.d.1.4.		09:00	B.H.Q moved to canal bank J25 d 14.	
		18:15	2 Coys of the 8th Batn were ordered to protect our Northern & Eastern flanks north units on our right and left were not level with us, thus reaching & Klairons of 'B' Coy on the west side, up to a line were forming a defensive flank 3000 yds N. of OIGNIES.	
		18:45	At 18:45 a short bombardment was put down on the Railway on J28 V39 units cases of which 'B' & 'C' Coys advanced and finally established themselves by 19:30 on the Railway on J28 & B. heavier A & D Coys were moved up in line up to, 'A' Coy to PINES, 'D' Coy to road J38 & 44. Reinforcements found as follows: 2 Lieut. L. R. Cam	
	11-10-18	05:30	Our dawn patrols were pushed in by 'B' 'C' Coys from the Railway then returned with the news that GORGETELLE was not held and that FOSSE I was empty. Immediately 'A' & 'D' Coys advanced through 'C' & 'B' Coys manoeuvring and advanced on THIMERES - BELLINCAMP Road & Railway on K31 & 39.	
J28 central			B.H.Q. moved to J28 central. The advance was carried out by Infantry 'B' & 'C' Coys moving up in close support D. Section being established in the hands of 'B' & 'D' Coys by the evening, to reconnoitre their front. 'B' & 'C' Coys were then ordered to form an support line in front of the main objective as follows:- 'C' Coy to hold the eastern outskirts of MONS-EN-PEVELLE to La VACQUERIE.	
			LA VACQUERIE to BUSSINCOURT with post in front. This was carried out by 'B' & 'C' Coys who were relieved in position by 1900. 'B' & D Coys being of the time relieved at K31 & 6.4. Remaining 2 Coys billets in LE THEUL.	
K27.a.6.4		19:00		

Army Form C. 2118.

WAR DIARY
or
INTELLIGENCE SUMMARY.
(Erase heading not required.)

Instructions regarding War Diaries and Intelligence Summaries are contained in F.S. Regs., Part II. and the Staff Manual respectively. Title pages will be prepared in manuscript.

Place	Date	Hour	Summary of Events and Information	Remarks and references to Appendices
KATAGNY	17-10-18		Still in contact with the enemy at VINCOURT & QUESNOY-LE-FERM. Lieut J.E. Forbes & Lieut G.S.J. Nicholls joined the Batln. the day with 6 Other Reinforcements	1821
	18-10-18	06.00	8th Batln passed through the Batln outpost line and the Batln was concentrated at MUSH EN-PEVELE in readiness to move at short notice	
		22.00	Batln less 2 Coys ("B" & "C" Coys) was ordered up to VINCOURT removing Bivouac stably at MONSECH-PEVELE. Move was complete by midnight and BHQ established L/13 d.4.2. Following reinforcements joined the Batln. 11 Other Ranks Maj. J.H.W. Bridge was posted to 2nd Bn KRRC and struck off strength of the Batln	
L.13.d.4.2.	19-10-18	06.15	2nd Bn. KRRC HQ at L.13.d.4.4. Batln with No. 1 Section "B" Coy, 58Bn M.G.C. Y 2 Guns 17th L.T.M.B, attacked VERCHAIN at 06.15 at X Roads L.19 & 5.0 forming the head of the main front. 8th Bn having passed through the 8th Bn. Batln to form advanced guard to the Brigade. Brigade pressed on steadily all day 8th Batln finally taking NOMAIN and 8th Batln was billeted at VERT BOIS.	M1
NOMAIN	20-10-18		Batln marched to NOMAIN at 11.00 on leaving VINCOURT 12.00 B.H.Q at G.12 a 2.8	
	21-10-18		Batln remained resting at NOMAIN. Any training was carried out during the morning	
	22-10-18	06.05	Orders were received that the Batln was to be ready to move at 1 hours notice after 10.00 This order was cancelled at 13.00 Batln further orders the Batln at 13.00 5 Officers 62 Other Ranks Major Bailey, 2 Lieuts Butler, Lumley, Forbes, Stafford. joined the Batln. Batln was ordered in readiness to move at 3 hours notice	

Army Form C. 2118.

WAR DIARY
or
INTELLIGENCE SUMMARY.
(Erase heading not required.)

Instructions regarding War Diaries and Intelligence Summaries are contained in F. S. Regs., Part II. and the Staff Manual respectively. Title pages will be prepared in manuscript.

Place	Date	Hour	Summary of Events and Information	Remarks and references to Appendices
NOMAIN	23-10-18		Battalion at NOMAIN resting. Reinforcements joined as follows 12 O. Ranks	
	24-10-18		Battalion remained at Nomain and carried out day training only	
	25-10-18			
	26-10-18	08.00	Message received Batt. were under one hours notice to move	G938
		10.00	Message received. Batt. would leave starting point 1100 on route J.21.d.1.0 & 23.b.3.5	2.9?
			Batt. via Rd. with the Bde towards BLÉHARIES but soon more orders were received to return to billets	
			Batt. was ordered to march to BOIS DE RONZY and take over the whole of the Right Batt. Sector	
			now held by 9th & 10th Btns 115th Inf. Bde. This was carried out and being completed by 21.30.	
			Batt. being disposed with 3 Coys in the front line, one on the right and B.H.Q. & one in support and Reserve.	
			Batt. sector was from J.10.a.5.8 to J.3.d.central along Scarpe and Railway.	
			Reinforcements joined as follows. 4 O. Ranks.	
			Our patrols maintained touch with the Enemy otherwise the day was quiet.	
			Ref. Sheet 44 NE 1/20,000	
CENSE DE CROQUES	28-10-18			
J.9.d.1.5	29-10-18		Reconnaissance carried out all day by Officers of "A" Coy in view of preparing the double in-	
			Capturing CHATEAU MORTAGNE and LEFOUT. Rd start and point on to this had been allotted. Areas	
			the afg. front on J.10.b & 9.b.by Attacked by 7th Bde also and moved up from CENSE DES MOQUES	
			Companies crossed Rl. Scarpe and one section of M.G.s and 2.L.TM. Bns. Crossed 25-29-10-18.	
			Re-commences joined as follows. 5 O.R.	
			The crossing was complete by 01.30. the Batta. camping from 8 to 10 men at a time. the RIVER being	
			concealed at this and Junc. The Rd was reported to Crossing H.Q. at 02.30. J.9.d.53 was reported	
	30-10-18		Vacated by the Russians at 01.45 and at 02.00 the Rd Running to Rd Junction at J.9.d.33 was	

Army Form C. 2118.

WAR DIARY
or
INTELLIGENCE SUMMARY.
(Erase heading not required.)

Instructions regarding War Diaries and Intelligence Summaries are contained in F. S. Regs., Part II. and the Staff Manual respectively. Title pages will be prepared in manuscript.

Place	Date	Hour	Summary of Events and Information	Remarks and references to Appendices
Sq.d.1.5	30-10-18		Both Platoons gained their objectives and 1 Lieut. Phillips proceeded to clean up the Brasseur. This was carried out and by dawn Plateau de Mofaye was in our hands and most of LE FORT except the N.E. corner. At dusk a morning mist rose & considerable assistance to this enterprise Casualties 2nd Lieut. B. Elthus wounded and missing. No other ranks killed. Reinforcements formed as follows & Bn.	
	31-10-18		Orders to G.103, G.104, G.105 are attached. Touch was maintained with the enemy all along the front by patrols. D.Coy relieved 1st Bn in the LE FORT - Rabour Monteney sep sector A by taking over positions vacated by D.Coy. A nights post was established on the Rive ESCAUT as S10 k34. Bn. was disposed as in Map A attached.	

[signature] Capt & Adjt.
7TH BATTN. THE LONDON REGT.

Army Form C. 2118.

WAR DIARY
or
INTELLIGENCE SUMMARY.

(Erase heading not required.)

Place	Date	Hour	Summary of Events and Information	Remarks and references to Appendices
IZQUIS	1-11-18		Strength 44 NS 1/2000. Key codes "A" 2/Lt Fenton, "B" 2/Lt Haddowner, "C" Lt A M. Leod, "D" Lt Gun. Hare.	
	2-11-18		On the night of 1/2nd Nov. the Batln was relieved by 3rd Batn. relief complete by 21.30 and returned to billets. 3 troops Rue Donnell and recently 1 troop 4 BHQ Canal de Roques.	
	3-11-18		Batn resting.	
	4-11-18		Batn resting. Bren gun platoon and grooms NCO's classes.	
	5-11-18		Batn resting. Jackals during night exercises.	
	6-11-18		Batn resting. Training under Troop arrangements M & P	
	7-11-18		Batn resting – 11.00 – drill.	
	8-11-18		On receipt of orders Batn marched out MAULDE 9.15 o'clock & arrived at El BARTE at 12.30 [illegible]	
MAULDE				
MORTAGNE	9-11-18	15.37	Batn. marched in march order to BRASMENIL one LO Batn wounded.	
BRASMENIL	10-11-18		Batn. marched in march order to BRASMENIL arriving at 15.45 1st Lt [illegible] to Brig [illegible] acting B.H.Q. in Rue L'Abbaye	
BELOEIL	11-11-18		Batn moved to GRASACE Hostilities ceased 11.00 hours Batn Hd [illegible] 1/5 19373	
GRASAGE				
	12-11-18		Batn moved to BIDERIE	
BIDERIE				
	13-11-18		Batn moved to BELOEIL BHQ at CHALEAD, Rue des [illegible]	
BELOEIL				
	14-11-18		Batn attended thanksgiving service.	

Army Form C. 2118.

WAR DIARY
or
INTELLIGENCE SUMMARY.
(Erase heading not required.)

Instructions regarding War Diaries and Intelligence Summaries are contained in F.S. Regs., Part II. and the Staff Manual respectively. Title pages will be prepared in manuscript.

Place	Date	Hour	Summary of Events and Information	Remarks and references to Appendices
BERLEL	15-11-18		Bath. Training and Educational training	
	16-11-18		Battn. Training and Educational training	
	17-11-18		Battn. attended Bde Church parade	
	18-11-18		Battn. moved by motor route to Berlin in PERUWELZ	
	19-11-18		Battn. Training and Education as usual	
	20-11-18		Battn. Training and Education	
	21-11-18		Battn. Training and Educational training	
	22-11-18		Battn. Training and Educational training	B.G.O. inspected Transport section of Battn.
	23-11-18		Battn. Training and Educational training	
	24-11-18		Battn. Training and Educational training	
	25-11-18		Battn. Training and Educational training	
	26-11-18		Battn. Training and Educational training	
	27-11-18		Battn. Training and Educational training	
	28-11-18		Battn. Training and Educational training	
	29-11-18		Battn. Training and Educational training	
	30-11-18		Battn. was inspected by B.G.O. 174 Inf Bde	

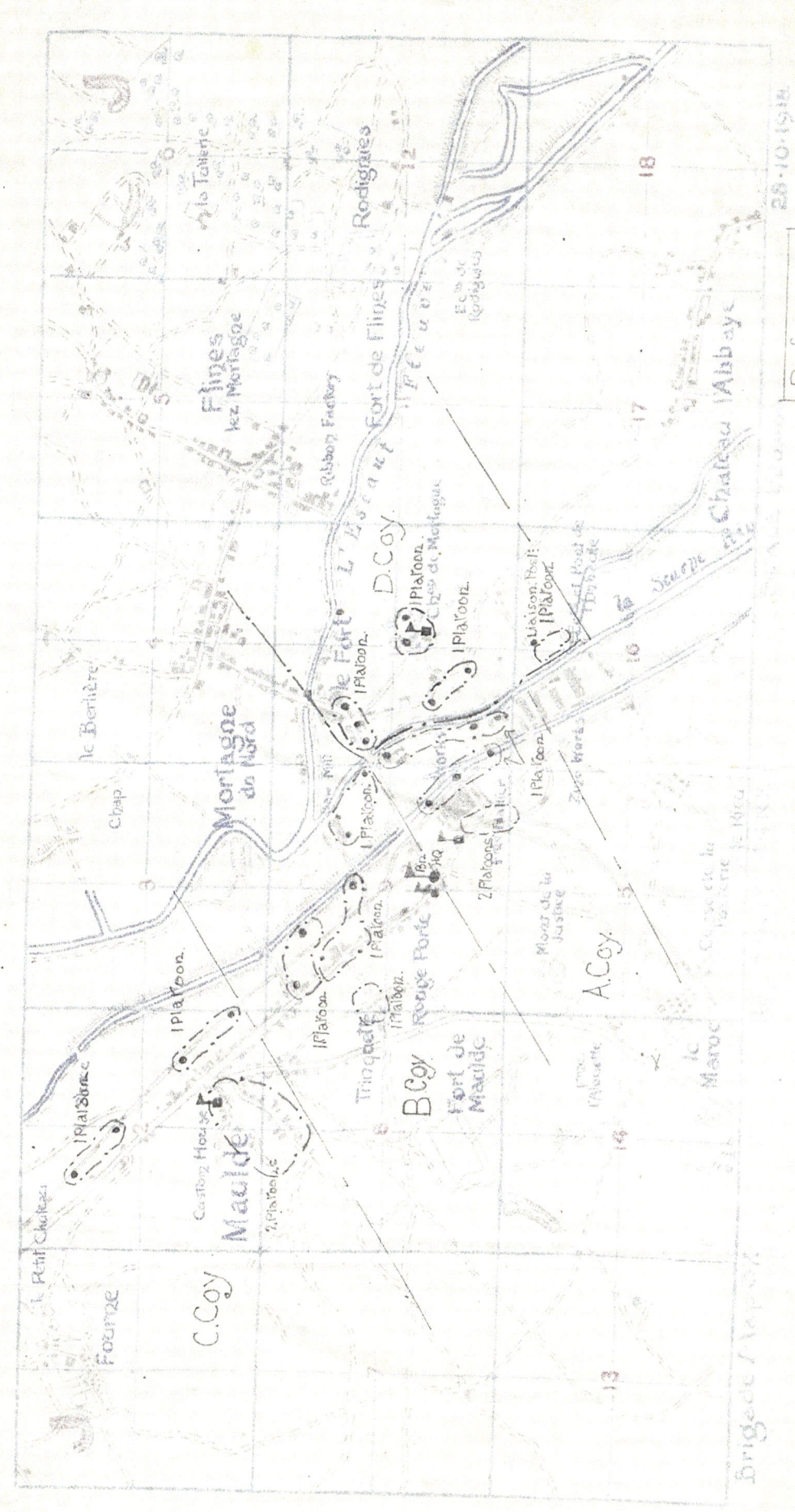

www.ingramcontent.com/pod-product-compliance
Lightning Source LLC
Chambersburg PA
CBHW081456160426
43193CB00013B/2497